Her new mummy and daddy had been talking to her about this yesterday, and told her she could talk to them if she had any worries. She liked her new parents. They were kind, they explained things and they always did what they said they would. Plus her daddy was very funny and often made her and Mummy laugh. She just hoped it would stay good. But because of how people had been in her past, she found it difficult to trust adults, and to trust that happy times could last.

When Kirsty turned round, she noticed that Billy was trying to plait his hair, but had knotted his finger in his plait. She giggled, **"You may be magic, but you still do silly things sometimes."**

They both laughed as Kirsty untangled him.

"**You know,**" Billy said, as he brushed himself down and settled himself comfortably on Kirsty's bed, "**when children have lived in families with problems, well, when they move, they have to learn all over again about how to live in a new family.**"

"**Yes,**" Kirsty agreed as she nodded vigorously, "**and it's not always easy and you don't always get it right,**" she added.

"**It takes practice,**" they both said at the very same time. "**Wow, we are even thinking the same things now!**" Kirsty said as she sat down next to Billy.

After a while Billy said gently, **"You know Kirsty, you really don't need me any more. You understand stuff now, and you are good at asking questions and talking about your worries. Plus, you have got your new family who are good at listening and are also very kind and caring."**

Kirsty nodded as a tear slipped down her cheek. She knew Billy was right, and that it was time for him to leave, but she felt sad about him going.

"Were you thinking about going back with Sara and George when they leave today?" Kirsty asked.

"What do you think about that idea?" Billy checked with her.

After some thought, Kirsty replied, **"I think it would be a good idea, because then you could help other children."**

Billy nodded.

"You know I would never forget you, and you will always have a special place in my heart," Billy said softly.

He went on, **"People who care about each other always remember each other, even when they are not together."**

"Do you think that my first mum and dad still think of me?" Kirsty asked.

"I'm sure they do," Billy replied.

"And do you think that my brothers think of me as well?"

"I'm sure they do and the good thing about your brothers is that you will get to see each other every year," he added.

Kirsty reached for her Life Story
Book and cuddled it to her.

DING DONG

"My new mummy and daddy are happy for me to talk about people who have been important to me and things that have happened to me, both good and bad. They said it helps them to get to know me better, and feel closer to me. That's good, isn't it?" Kirsty asked.

"Yes, that's very good," Billy agreed.

Then the doorbell rang.

"Kirsty darling, Sara and George are here, do you want to come down?" they heard her mummy call.

Kirsty and Billy both had a cuddle before getting up to go downstairs. They were smiling as they walked into the front room. Although bad stuff had happened in the past, they both had a feeling that there would be lots of good times ahead.